THE
AMAZING BANANA
COOKBOOK

by

Adam Starchild

Creative Cookbooks
Monterey, California

The Amazing Banana Cookbook

by
Adam Starchild

ISBN: 1-4101-0707-8

Copyright © 2004 by Fredonia Books

Creative Cookbooks
An Imprint of Fredonia Books
Monterey, California
http://www.creativecookbooks.com

THE AMAZING BANANA COOKBOOK

by

Adam Starchild

Co-author of The Seafood Cookbook

CONTENTS

INTRODUCTION

Have you ever paused to consider that the banana is one of nature's most versatile, delectable and nutritious foods? At the same time, the banana is a food which Americans take for granted and about which they know very little.

• The banana "tree"—which is not a tree at all, but a giant plant—gives up its life to produce only one bunch of bananas. Bananas appear on the plant at about twelve months, and about three months later, are ready for reaping. In reaping, the plant is cut down, the reaper catches the banana bunch as the plant falls, and cuts it from the plant with a single stroke of his machete.

• In some parts of the banana—producing world, primitive methods are still used in the reaping and transporting of bananas to shipping points. In Jamaica, for instance, it is not unusual to see bananas being transported in lorries or mule carts—or even on people's heads—to shipping points, where they may be passed by hand through a port and into the ship's hold. Banana bunches are always carefully handled to avoid bruising.

• There are two basic types of bananas—those that are to be eaten raw as fruit, and those that are to be used for cooking. The cooking banana, which is not tasty to the American palate when eaten raw, is greatly improved in flavor by cooking. It usually has a skin of a deeper yellow than that of the eating banana, and the fruit is thicker and stubbier. Cooking bananas are not widely available in U.S. markets, and when you find them they will be in the vegetable display.

• The picking of bananas green is not done—as many Americans believe—at the expense of quality and flavor. Bananas are picked green even when they are to be eaten in the area where they are grown, because if a banana is left to ripen on the plant, the skin will break, the fruit will be attacked by insects, and the flavor and quality will be spoiled. If you buy bananas green or not quite ripe, you can ripen them at home in room temperature. Bananas do not ripen well or develop top flavor in refrigeration, but sliced bananas may be kept in the refrigerator before using them in salads. (A good way to preserve the flavor and color of banana slices is by dipping them in citrus juices or a solution of ascorbic acid.)

• The banana has five stages of ripening, and it can be used for some purpose in four of those stages:

—In the *first* stage, the banana is green, and should be left to ripen.

—In the *second* stage, it will be yellow with a green tip, and is just right for baking, broiling or frying; cooking brings out a distinctive flavor.

—In the *third* stage it will be all yellow, at which time it is good for eating raw, but still firm enough for cooking.

—In the *fourth* stage it is yellow with brown flecks—indicating that the starches are turning to fruit sugars—and is just right for a child's lunch box.

—In the *fifth* stage, the banana is more dark than yellow, and our grandmothers have for many years used this inexpensive, nutritionally excellent fruit for making banana bread and banana butter.

• The average banana, as purchased, contains the following nutrients:

75.00	calories
.97	grams protein
.17	grams fat
19.57	grams of carbohydrate
7.14	milligrams of calcium
22.85	milligrams of phosphorus
.62	milligrams of iron
.85	milligrams of sodium
326.00	milligrams of potassium
168.50	International Units Vitamin A
.04	milligrams thiamine
.05	milligrams riboflavin
.62	milligrams niacin
8.85	milligrams ascorbic acid

With the high potassium content, fair ratio of protein to carbohydrates, good fibrous content and moderate calories, the tasty banana can be a welcome part of any diet that allows carbohydrates.

This book tells you the many ways to prepare this tasty and exotic food

— The Amazing Banana.

BANANA APPETIZERS

Banana Appetizer
Serves 6.

2 cups mashed ripe
  bananas
1 tsp. lime juice

1 pt. pineapple juice
  (sweetened)
6 whole cherries

Mix mashed banana with pineapple juice. Add lime juice. Pour over cracked ice. Garnish with cherries. Serve in cocktail glasses.

Banana Cheese Dip

8 oz. cream cheese
4 tbs. milk
1 tbs. sherry
¾ tsp. curry powder

3 tbs. chopped chutney
1 cup diced ripe banana
Potato chips or crackers

Blend together cream cheese, milk and sherry until light and fluffy. Add curry powder and chutney to mixture. Fold in diced banana. Serve with chips or crackers.

Banana and Bacon Skewer
Serves 2.

1 banana
Cinnamon sugar

2 strips bacon cut in
  halves
1 orange

Cut banana in 4 crosswise. Turn in cinnamon sugar. Wrap each piece in half a bacon strip. Peel orange, removing outside pith. Cut into quarters. Sprinkle with cinnamon sugar. Arrange on skewer—banana, orange, banana, orange. Broil for 5 minutes.

6

Banana Canapes Serves 6.

6 ripe bananas
1 tbs. light rum
6 slices white bread

6 thin slices cheese (cut smaller than bread)
Butter, pepper

Purée bananas. Add rum and a sprinkle of pepper. Butter bread on one side and spread purée on it. Place on flat sheet and put in moderate oven until banana is heated through and begins to bubble. Then place a slice of cheese on each and return to oven until cheese has melted.

Banana Balls

Cream ripe banana and cheese; season to taste with mustard, horseradish, etc. Shape into small balls and roll in finely chopped parsley, chives, nuts, or in potato chips.

"Scratch-Me-Back" Cocktail Serves 2.

1 ripe banana
½ slice pineapple
½ slice papaya
 (or honeydew melon)
3 oz. sweetened condensed milk

3 oz. evaporated milk
3 oz. rum
Ice
Nutmeg

Peel banana, papaya and pineapple. Slice them and blend together in blender. Add milk and rum, then add ice and blend again. Serve sprinkled with grated nutmeg.

Banana Pizza

Serves 8-10.

9 oz. short crust pastry	1 green sweet pepper, diced
2 lbs. green bananas	
Salt	1 salad tomato, diced
1 hot pepper	3 strips bacon, finely chopped
Scallion	
Fat	½ cup grated cheese
1 cup diced cooked ham	

Line 9" pie tin with short crust pastry. Boil bananas with salt and hot pepper. Mash. Sauté finely chopped scallion in fat. Add to banana. Place mixture in pie shell and cover with ham, pepper, tomato and bacon. Sprinkle with grated cheese. Bake in hot oven for 15 minutes. Serve hot.

"Dip and Come Back" Dip

12 green bananas	Juice of 4 limes or
6 cups water	lemons
4 tbs. salt	

Peel and cut green bananas in halves, then lengthwise in quarters. Leave to soak in salted water and lime juice while the sauce is being prepared. After sauce is prepared dry banana in towel and fry in deep hot fat until brown. Drain. Arrange on a large platter with tomato hot sauce dip in bowl in center.

Tomato Hot Sauce Dip

2 cups canned whole	2 tbs. flour
tomatoes (app. 1 lb.)*	½ tsp. salt
1 small onion, sliced	1 tsp. Worcestershire
2 tbs. butter	sauce

Cook tomatoes and onion 10 minutes. Melt butter and sift in flour and salt. Stir over low flame. Add tomato mixture. Cook 2 minutes. Stir. Strain through fine sieve and add Worcestershire sauce.

*Note: Fresh salad tomatoes can be used but must be peeled and cooked for 25 minutes. Add ½ tsp. more salt and a little water.

9

BANANAS IN SOUPS

Banana and Fish Tea   Serves 6.

12 green bananas
2 onions
5 lbs. fresh fish

1 hot pepper
Scallion and thyme

Peel bananas. Place bananas, fish and other ingredients in boiling water to cover. Keep pot tightly covered. Cook for one hour. Serve hot.

Ironoh Broth   Serves 7.

7 green bananas
1 lb. fresh shrimps
   (peeled & deveined)
1½ tsp. salt
1 sprig thyme

2 bird peppers (or 2
   tsp. chili powder)
4 tsp. pickappa sauce*
1 cooking tomato
1 onion

Peel 4 bananas and let 3 remain unpeeled. Cut bananas in two. Put shrimps in 1½ qts. boiling water, add salt and let boil for one minute. Skim. Add unpeeled bananas and let boil for 2½ minutes. Add peeled bananas, chopped tomato, onion, peppers, thyme. Add sauce. Allow to cook for 15-20 minutes. Remove skin from unpeeled bananas. Serve with two pieces of banana to each cup.

*Note: Worchestershire sauce with a dash of paprika may be used instead.

Banana "Mars" Soup   Serves 6.

1 large beef bone or
2 lbs. stewing beef
14 green bananas
Milk from 3 coconuts
1 lb. tomatoes

2 stalks scallion
1 clove garlic
4 Irish potatoes
Salt, pepper, thyme to
   taste

Put beef or bone in 4 qts. water and cook for
4 hours to make stock. Blanch bananas in cold
water brought to boil. Dice potatoes, tomatoes,
chop scallion and garlic; add to beef stock.
Reduce stock by half and add diced bananas.
Add salt, pepper and thyme and coconut milk.
Cook for 5 minutes longer. Serve hot.

Banana Bisque   Serves 6.

½ lb. corned beef
4 cups stock
4 cups chopped boiled
  green bananas

1 cup minced onions
1 tsp. salt
¼-½ tsp. pepper
1 cup cream

Combine all ingredients. Bring to a boil and
simmer until bananas are pulpy (approximately
30–40 minutes). Rub through fine sieve; add
cream. Reheat to blend (do not boil). Serve
garnished with parsley or chives.

BANANA ENTREES

SEAFOOD

Banana and Shrimp Curry   Serves 2.

2 ripe bananas   3 cups curry sauce°
1½ tsp. butter   1 stalk scallion
3 oz. shrimps   1 green pepper
¾ cup cooked white rice ½ cup diced tomatoes

Peel banana. Place in baking dish. Brush well
with butter. Pour half the curry sauce over banana. Bake in moderate oven 10-15 minutes.
Cook shrimps in remaining curry sauce, add
seasoning and serve with the banana on a bed
of hot rice.

*To make Curry Sauce:

2 cups chicken broth   1 tbs. curry powder
1/3 cup coconut milk

Combine broth, coconut milk and curry powder.
Heat while stirring until sauce bubbles.

Banana Witch   Serves 6.

6 green bananas   24 green cucumbers*
1 coconut   12 shrimps, cleaned
1½ pts. water   1 tbs. tomato catsup
1 tsp. salt   1 tsp. ground black
1 stalk scallion   pepper
1 sprig thyme   1 hot pepper

Grate coconut. Add ¼ cup water to extract
milk. Put milk to boil for 15 minutes, then put
in bananas, cucumbers, shrimps and hot pepper.
When nearly cooked, add salt, catsup, scallion,
thyme and black pepper. Simmer for a few
minutes.

*Or 12 large cucumbers cut in halves.

Banana Sally   Serves 4.

¼ lb. codfish, flaked   2 green bananas, grated
1 onion, finely chopped   2-3 tbs. coconut cream**
1 tsp. black pepper   4 tbs. sifted flour
½ hot pepper, finely   1 egg
  chopped   Fat for frying
Sprig of thyme   2 tsp. baking powder

Season codfish with onion, black pepper and
thyme. Add coconut cream and half of the flour.
Add grated green banana. Add slightly beaten
egg mixture, blending thoroughly. Combine
remaining flour with baking powder and add to
mixture. Mix well. Drop by spoonful into very
hot fat. Fry till crisp and brown on both sides.

**Or use thick whipped cream.

13

Shrimp Luncheon Dish   Serves 4.

3 tbs. butter or margarine
1 onion, minced
1 green pepper, minced
1 clove garlic, minced
1 cup cooked rice
½ cup diced ripe banana
1½ cups shrimps, cleaned
1 tsp. salt
1 bay leaf
2 cups pineapple juice

Marinate banana in pineapple juice for 10 minutes. Melt butter or margarine in pan on medium heat, add all other ingredients. Cover and simmer for 30 minutes. Serve hot.

Friday Pie   Serves 6.

4 cups mashed boiled green banana
3 cups prepared mackerel*
Butter

Using 8″ or 9″ pie dish make pie shell with half of the mashed banana. Fill with prepared mackerel. Top with remaining mashed banana. Dot the top lightly with butter and bake in moderate oven until top is brown.

*Note: To prepare mackerel, wash and boil mackerel. Flake. Chop onion, tomato and pepper. Sauté. Combine with mackerel.

14

King Fish "Look Behind"

King fish cutlets   (Quantities as desired)
Salt, pepper   „
Butter   „
Ripe banana   „
Mustard sauce*   „

Season cutlets with salt and pepper. Fry in butter. Cover each cutlet with ripe banana slices. Top each cutlet with a slice of cheddar cheese. Put under broiler till cheese is melted and banana hot. Serve mustard sauce on the side.

*To make mustard sauce:

Melt 5 oz. butter, add 2 oz. flour. Fill up with fish stock to approx. ¼ pt. Add mustard to taste. Season with salt and lime juice.

MEATS

Chicken Cayman Style   Serves 4.

4 1-lb. chickens	6 cooked prunes
6 green bananas	1 large papaya melon (or honeydew melon)

Boil bananas and mash. Mix with chopped prunes, and stuff birds with mixture. Cook in oven 350°F. Cut papaya in quarters lengthwise. Dress cooked birds in papaya sections. Garnish as desired.

Roast Suckling Pig
with Apple-Banana Purée

Serves 8-10.

Prepare pig for roasting, using desired stuffing.
Serve with apple-banana purée.

Apple-Banana Purée

1 (16 oz.) can apple   2 cloves
sauce   1 tsp. cinnamon
6 ripe bananas

Purée ripe banana. Combine with apple sauce.
Add cloves and cinnamon. Mix well.

Baked Chicken
with Banana Stuffing

Serves 6-8.

1 6–lb. roasting chicken   ¼ tsp. salt
¼ cup finely chopped   2¼ cups soft bread
   onions   crumbs, firmly packed
¼ tsp. poultry seasoning   ½ cup melted butter or
1½ cups diced ripe   margarine
   banana

Prepare chicken for roasting. Follow recipe for
stuffing as set out. Put in greased uncovered
roast pan in oven at 350°F. for approx. 1½
hours or until done.

Banana Meat Loaf
Serves 4-6.

1 lb. ground beef   ¼ tsp. pepper
1 tbs. chopped onion   ½ tsp. dry mustard
1 cup bread crumbs   2 cups mashed ripe
1 tbs. salt   banana

Combine meat, onion, salt, pepper and bread crumbs. Add mustard to banana. Stir into meat mixture. Form into loaf and bake in loaf pan, at 350°F. for about 1 hour. Serve with desired sauce.

Ham Steak "Ocho Rios"
Serves 1

Take a thick slice of ham. Make an opening in the ham by cutting from the side halfway through thickness. Cut a ripe banana in halves lengthwise and place both halves inside opening. Broil until done. Top with a fried egg. Serve with hot Banana Pancakes. (*See* page 54.)

Duck A La Banane

Serves 6-8.

1 5-lb. duck (pre-
  pared for cooking)
3 firm ripe bananas for
  stuffing
Ripe bananas for
  garnishing

½ cup bread crumbs
½ cup raisins
½ cup mango nectar
  (or peach nectar)
2 tsp. corn flour

Mash bananas until smooth, add bread crumbs and raisins. Fill duck cavity with stuffing, and truss. Prick duck with fork, roast breast side up on wire rack at 325°F. for approximately 2 hours. Add corn flour to mango nectar, boil until clear, allow to cool. Garnish with ripe banana slices coating garnish with cooled mango glaze.

Banana Home—Style

Serves 4.

¼ lb. cod fish
8 green bananas
½ tsp. salt
1 onion
1 small cucumber
1 carrot

1 small bundle callaloo
  or spinach
1 oz. melted butter
1 salad tomato
¼ lb. salt pork

Soak pork and fish in cold water. Boil bananas and mash while hot. Brush with melted butter and make into balls. Chop spinach finely. Clean and flake fish. Cut pork into small cubes. Fry fish and pork together. Combine with spinach, salt and onion. Steam until spinach is tender. Arrange on platter with banana balls around. Garnish with sliced carrot, tomato and cucumber.

Pork Loin Downtown

Serves 4-6.

Loin of Pork
Ripe bananas
Seasoning

2 cups boiled green
  banana purée
½ cup sliced almonds
½ cup sautéd onions

Debone and defat pork loin. Stuff as many ripe bananas through the whole as will hold. Season well. Roast. Cut in slices. Combine green banana pureé, sliced almonds and sautéd onions. Spread on platter. Arrange pork loin slices over. Cover with a Sauce Piquante.*

*To make Sauce Piquante: Finely chopped hot pepper, dill pickles, and anchovies; combine and season with salt, pepper and mustard. Mix well with brown gravy from the pork.

Banana Shepherd's Pie   Serves 8.

1 doz. green bananas	1 green sweet pepper
1 lb. mince	Salt and pepper
¼ lb. butter	3 oz. shredded cheese
4 tbs. cooking oil	1 cup unsweetened milk
1 cup bread crumbs	Paprika
2 onions	

Brown mince in 4 tablespoons oil; add chopped onions, garlic, sweet pepper and 1 cup boiling water; cover for 10 minutes over a medium heat then add ¾ cup boiling water, 1 oz. butter and ½ cup bread crumbs; leave to simmer for 15 minutes. Boil bananas, add salt to taste and cream to a smooth paste, with remaining butter and milk.

Place mince mixture in a greased casserole dish and top with layers of bread crumbs, banana paste and grated cheese in that order, and top with remaining bread crumbs. Bake in oven 350°F. for 25 minutes.

Baked Chicken Mt. Diablo　　Serves 6-10.

1 3-lb. chicken	½ cup flour
1 tsp. salt	½ cup milk
1 tsp. ginger	1 cup bread crumbs
Fat for frying	3 ripe bananas

Cut chicken into serving pieces. Season well with salt, pepper and ginger. Dredge chicken pieces in flour. Dip in milk and coat with bread crumbs. Fry in hot fat until almost done. Place in slightly greased uncovered roast pan. Slice bananas in halves, then lengthwise; slice tomato and arrange in pan with chicken and bananas. Bake at 350°F. for approx. ½ hour or until done.

Bahamas Special

Veal cutlets	(Quantities as desired)
Beef tenderloin	,,
Ripe bananas	,,
Onion	,,
Sweet pepper	,,
Shredded coconut	,,
Pineapple or mango	,,
slices	
Mayonnaise	,,
1 or 2 eggs, well beaten	

Cut veal cutlets and beef tenderloin into thin strips. Cut ripe bananas in medium-sized pieces. Cut onion rings, green pepper rings. Dip all ingredients in egg and then in shredded coconut. Deep fry and serve dry, with mayonnaise and mango or pineapple slices.

BANANA AS VEGETABLE AND IN SALADS

Cooking bananas, or plantains, are excellent served as a vegetable. They may be baked, boiled or sautéed.

Baked: Leave plantains in skins. Wash and place in a baking pan or on aluminum foil in oven. Bake at 350°F. about 30-40 minutes or until banana is easily pierced with a fork. Skins may split during baking. Stir skins lengthwise; season with margarine and brown sugar, or salt and pepper. Serve hot as a vegetable in place of potato or rice.

Boiled: Leave plantains in skins. Wash, then cook in boiling water 15-20 minutes. Drain. Slit lengthwise and serve as a baked banana.

Sautéed: Use either the eating type banana or plantain. The Brazilian banana is excellent served sautéed, as it retains its shape and color. Peel the bananas. Melt margarine or butter in heavy skillet, and cook bananas slowly until slightly brown. Add guava jelly and lemon juice or sherry, and spoon mixture over bananas until they are glazed. Serve hot with a meat course, or curry, or as a dessert.

Scalloped Bananas Au Gratin   Serves 6-8.

4 cups thinly-sliced peeled green banana	2 cups medium white sauce*
1 cup thinly-sliced onions	1 cup grated cheddar cheese
1 pat butter	Salt and pepper

Cook sliced bananas in small quantity of boiling salted water for 10 minutes. Drain and arrange in alternate layers with onions in greased 1½ qt. casserole. Pour white sauce over, sprinkle with cheese, dot with butter and bake uncovered in moderate oven for approx. 45 minutes, or till banana is tender.

*To make white sauce:

4 tbs. butter or margarine	Few grains pepper
4 tbs. flour	Few grains paprika
1 tsp. salt	2 cups milk

Melt butter or margarine in sauce pan over low heat. Blend in flour, salt, paprika, pepper. Stir until smooth. Remove from heat. Gradually blend in milk. Return to direct medium heat and stir constantly until smoothly thickened. Add more seasoning if desired.

Rice Banana   Serves 4-6.

6 green bananas   1 pt. water
2 tbs. butter   Salt to taste

Peel bananas. Cut in halves. Cook in boiling salted water. When cooked, rice with a ricer; add butter.

Fried Ripe Bananas   Serves 5-6.

10 firm ripe bananas   2 tbs. milk
 2 eggs   2 tbs. flour
 1 pt. oil

Peel bananas and roll them in flour. Whip eggs with milk. Dip bananas in liquid. Drain slightly. Drop in hot fat. Turn often until brown. Serve hot.

Banana Nut Salad   Serves 4-6.

3 ripe bananas   ½ cup sour cream
1 head lettuce   ½ cup chopped nuts

Slice bananas. Arrange lettuce leaves in salad bowl. Place banana slices on top. Mix sour cream and spread over bananas. Top with chopped nuts.

Banana En Casserole

3 sweet potatoes
3 - 5 ripe bananas
8 gingersnap cookies,
  crushed
2 tbs. butter

2 oz. raisins
⅓ cup orange juice
⅓ cup water
2 tbs. sugar

Cook potatoes. Peel and slice ¼" thick. Peel and slice bananas. Arrange alternate layers of potatoes, bananas, crumbs and raisins in casserole. Dot layers with butter. Boil together orange juice, water and sugar. Pour over layers. Bake covered in a hot oven 400°F. for 25 minutes. Uncover and allow to brown. Serve with ham or roast pork.

Banana Au Gratin   Serves 6.

12 green bananas	1 cup grated cheese
2 cups milk	2 eggs slightly beaten
¼ cup melted butter	½ tsp. salt
2 tsp. cinnamon	

Boil bananas until cooked. Mash. Add milk,
butter, cinnamon, eggs, salt and ¾ cup cheese.
Mix well. Put into a greased baking dish;
sprinkle the rest of cheese on top. Bake for 15
minutes in a slow oven. Garnish with parsley.

Banana and Pineapple Salad
with Lemon French Dressing*   Serves 4-6.

4 ozs. cheddar cheese	2 tbs. pineapple juice
4 slices pineapple	3 ripe bananas
½ oz. butter	Lettuce

Grate cheese. Add pineapple juice and soft butter to cheese. Beat until creamy. Slice bananas
lengthwise. Spread with cheese mixture. Arrange fruit on lettuce bed and garnish with
cherries.

*To make lemon french dressing:

½ cup salad oil	Cayenne
½ cup lemon juice	2 tbs. honey or sugar
½ tsp. salt	

Combine all ingredients and shake well before
using.

28

German Salad   Serves 4.

4 ripe bananas sliced   1 tbs. unflavoured
½ cup chopped cherries   gelatine
1 tbs. custard powder

Dissolve gelatine in 1 cup hot water. Cool. Mix
in custard powder. Add sliced bananas and
cherries. Put in a bowl and place in refrigerator
to set: Unmold. Decorate with green and red
cherries, black olives and dill pickles.

Banana indiani   Serves 4-6.

3 cups sliced green   2 tbs. bread crumbs
  banana   1 tsp. lemon juice
3 cups water   1 tbs. mango chutney
3 tsp. gelatine   (or strong, sweet relish)
1 tbs. curry powder   1 tsp. salt

Mix curry powder, salt and lemon juice. Put
banana and curry mixture into water to cook.
Add chutney, crumbs and dissolved gelatine.
Place in mould and allow to set. Garnish with
red sweet peppers.

Honeymoon Hearts   Serves 6.

6 hearts of lettuce   1 tsp. curry powder
3 ripe bananas   ½ cup mayonnaise

Slice bananas in rounds. Blend curry powder
with mayonnaise. Add banana slices to mixture.
Place inside hearts of lettuce.

Banana Puff   Serves 6.

6 green bananas	½ tsp. salt
1 - 2 tbs. milk	½ tsp. pepper
1 tbs. butter	1 egg yolk

Peel and boil bananas. While bananas are hot, drain and mash until smooth. Put in a saucepan. Add egg yolk, milk and butter. Heat over low flame until mixture is light and leaves the sides of the pan. Put in a forcing bag with large rosette. Pipe individual puffs onto a greased baking tin. Brush with a little milk and bake in a hot oven until golden brown. Serve hot.

Banana Mossah   Serves 6.

6 green bananas	1 salad tomato
2 coconuts, grated	1 sprig thyme
1 onion	½ tsp. salt
1 hot pepper	2 pods annatto
Scallion	(optional)

Extract coconut milk. Place in saucepan over medium heat and bring to boil. Add peeled green bananas. Add remaining ingredients. Let cook until the coconut becomes a custard.

BANANA DESSERTS

Banana Cream Pie   **one 9" inch pie.**

One of the most popular of all pies, combining a rich, creamy filling with mellow, fully ripe bananas.

½ cup sugar
¼ teaspoon salt
¼ cup cornstarch or
⅓ cup flour
1 pint milk, scalded
2 eggs slightly beaten

1 tablespoon butter or
  margarine
½ teaspoon vanilla
1 baked 9" pie shell
3 ripe bananas

Mix sugar. salt and cornstarch or flour. Gradually add to milk. Stir over low heat until thick. Stir a small amount of hot mixture into eggs. Then pour back into remaining hot mixture while beating. Continue cooking about 2 minutes or until thickened. Remove from heat. Add butter or margarine and vanilla. Cool thoroughly. Hot fillings change the flavor of bananas. Line pie shell with layer of cooled filling. Slice bananas over filling. Cover immediately with remaining filling. Top with whipped cream and banana slices, if desired.

Quickie Bananas   Serves 4

½ lb. sugar
½ pt. water
3 ripe bananas

Nutmeg
bitters
Crystallized ginger

Dissolve sugar in water and boil until as thick
as honey. Cut bananas lengthwise and place in
liquid. Cool. Sprinkle with nutmeg, few drops
of bitters, and decorate with ginger. Serve cold.

Fiesta **Banana** Cake   8" layer cake.

2 cups cake flour, sifted	½ cup shortening
1 teaspoon baking powder	½ cup sour milk or buttermilk
1 teaspoon baking soda	1 cup mashed ripe bananas
¾ teaspoon salt	
2 eggs, unbeaten	1 teaspoon vanilla
1⅓ cups sugar	½ cup chopped nuts

Measure flour, baking powder, soda, salt and sugar into sifter. Place shortening in mixing bowl; stir to soften. Sift in dry ingredients. Add ¼ cup milk and mashed bananas. Mix until flour is dampened. Beat 2 minutes in mixer (at low speed) or 300 vigorous strokes by hand. Add the eggs, vanilla, nuts, and remaining milk. Beat 1 minute more. Pour into two round 8" layer pans, lined with paper on bottoms. Bake in moderate oven (350°F) about 35 to 40 minutes. Cool. Spoon whipped cream between layers and on top of cake. Garnish with banana slices.

Banana Brazilian   Serves 6.

¼ cup confectioner's sugar	6 ripe bananas
1 tbs. cocoa	Chopped Brazil nuts

Sift together sugar and cocoa. Peel bananas. Roll in sugar mixture. Chill. Sprinkle with chopped nuts. Top with cream.

Banana Sunset
Serves 8-10.

8 ripe bananas
½ lbs. sugar
½ lb. flour
3 oz. raisins
1 oz. mixed nuts
2 oz. cherries
¼ tsp. lime juice

½ tsp. vanilla
½ lb. butter
4 tsp. baking powder
4 eggs
¾ pt. milk
½ cup grated coconut

Cream bananas and sugar; add eggs beaten well; add milk and flour, mix well; add raisins, cherries and nuts. Mix in rest of ingredients except coconut. Turn out mixture in 9" baking tin. Bake at 400°F. for 1 hour 20 minutes. Turn out and cool. Cover top with whipped cream and coconut, decorate with sliced oranges.

Banana Jonkanoo Pie
Serves 6-8.

1½ cups milk
3 eggs
3 tbs. cornstarch

6 oz. sugar
5 ripe bananas, puréed

Boil milk with sugar. Mix cornstarch with ½ cup cold milk and the egg yolks. Add to rest of milk and cook for 5 minutes. Add banana purée and pour into a baked pie shell. Beat egg whites to which a little sugar has been added until stiff. Form meringue over top. Grill for 2 minutes. Decorate as desired.

34

Banana Pineapple Merinque   Serves 6.

3 ripe bananas .... 1 tsp. nutmeg
2 eggs .... 1 can crushed pineapple
2 tbs. sugar .... 1 tbs. rum

Purée bananas and rub in unbeaten egg yolks,
1 tbs. sugar and nutmeg. Place in shallow pie
dish. Cover with drained pineapple. Beat egg
whites until stiff enough to stand in peaks, adding rum and remaining sugar. Pile over pineapple and bake in oven until golden brown.

Banana Parfait   Serves 5.

5 eggs .... ½ cup rum
½ pt. cream .... 1 tbs. unflavoured
¼ lb. sugar ....   gelatine
½ pt. banana purée .... 1 tsp. vanilla

Whip cream. Mix egg with sugar, fold in banana
purée and whipped cream. Dissolve gelatine in
rum and add vanilla. Pour in parfait glasses and
freeze. Decorate with whipped cream and ripe
banana slices.

Banana Whip   Serves 2-4.

½ cup banana purée .... 2 egg whites
1 pkt. lime flavoured ..... ½ cup sugar
   gelatine

Partially set gelatine. Whip. Add banana purée.
Whip egg whites until stiff, add sugar. Fold in
all together, set in glass mould. Chill. Decorate
with cherries and whipped cream.

Banana Ice Cream

Yields 1 quart.

1 pt. milk	¾ cup evaporated milk
1 tbs. custard powder	½ cup sweetened
2 egg yolks	condensed milk
	3 bananas, puréed

Mix custard powder to a paste with a little of the milk. Bring remainder of milk to boil and stir in paste and beaten egg yolks. Cook over low flame for 3 minutes. Stir until cool then mix in condensed and evaporated milk and banana purée. Allow to freeze. When very firm pack in container lined with wax paper; leave edge to overhang. Cover. Store in freezer.

Banana Betty

Serves 4-6.

⅓ cup melted butter	½ cup raisins
1 cup bread or cake	¼ tsp. cinnamon
crumbs	1 tsp. grated lime rind
3 ripe bananas, sliced	2 tbs. lime juice
½ cup sugar	¼ cup water
½ tsp. nutmeg	

Combine crumbs, raisins, sugar, nutmeg and cinnamon. Arrange banana slices and crumb mixture in layers in greased 1-quart ovenware dish. Combine butter and lime juice and pour over top layer. Sprinkle the last of the crumb mixture on top. Bake until brown. Serve with coconut cream.

Banana Cake

Serves 4-6.

½ cup butter
1 cup sugar
2 eggs
3 ripe bananas, puréed
2 cups flour

½ tsp. nutmeg
1 tsp. bicarbonate of soda
½ cup chopped cashew nuts

Cream butter and sugar; beat in eggs one at a time. Fold in mashed bananas and flour sifted with soda and nutmeg. Add cashew nuts. Bake about 50 minutes in lined, greased cake tin.

Deep Dish Banana and Apple Conserve

Serves 6.

2 lbs. ripe bananas, sliced lengthwise	1 cup sugar
	1½ cups cornstarch
2 tbs. rum	1 tsp. salt
1 lb. apples, sliced	¼ lbs. butter
2 tbs. honey	2 tbs. lemon juice

Arrange banana and apple slices in baking dish. Combine sugar, rum, cornstarch, salt, honey and lemon juice. Pour over banana and apple. Dot with butter. Bake at 400°F. for 45 minutes. Serve with cinnamon whipped cream. Top with chopped nuts.

Devil's Horn

Serves 4-6.

1 lb. puff pastry	1 cup cream
1 qt. custard cream*	2 tsp. unflavoured gelatine
1 cup banana purée	

Roll puff pastry, cut in long slices, roll into horn shape; bake for 20 minutes. Blend custard cream, banana purée, cream and gelatine. Fill pastry horn with mixture.

*To make custard cream: Mix custard powder with cold milk to yield 1 pt. Boil until set.

Banana Cheese Cake
Serves 8-10

1½ lb. cream cheese   1 orange
4 eggs   2 tsp. vanilla
4 oz. sugar   Nutmeg
½ cup cream   Banana jam*

Mix cream cheese with sugar; add cream and grated rind of orange. Add vanilla, nutmeg and eggs. Cook in a double-boiler for 45 minutes. Put in mould to set. Unmould when cool. Put a topping of banana jam and decorate with whipped cream and ripe banana.

*Banana jam: *See* page 53.

Banana Trifle A La Spaniard
Serves 4-6.

1 pt. milk   1 tsp. vanilla
3 egg yolks   5 ripe bananas, sliced
4 oz. custard powder   6 oz. sugar

Boil milk. Mix custard powder and egg yolks with ½ cup boiled milk. Add mixture to rest of boiled milk, and cook for 4 minutes. Put sliced bananas in serving glasses. Pour cream custard over and put to chill. Decorate with a biscuit, whipped cream and a cherry.

Banana Baked Alaska

This dessert is made with hard-frozen ice cream set on banana cake, covered with meringue and placed in a hot oven until meringue browns.

Set banana ice cream to freeze in a container lined with waxed paper. The container should be of exactly the same proportions as the tin in which banana cake is baked. Make banana cake for base of dessert (see page 39). Make meringue*. Meringue must be ready to spread immediately when ice cream is unmoulded.

When ready to serve—Remove banana cake from pan and place on pastry board which has been completely covered with aluminum foil. Unmould ice cream, peel off paper. Set ice cream on cake. Spread meringue to cover ice cream and cake, sealing edges carefully. Pipe left-over meringue through forcing bag to decorate. Place in hot oven 3-5 minutes until meringue is light brown.

*To make Meringue:
1 cup granulated sugar 4 egg whites
2 tbs. light rum

Beat egg whites, add sugar and rum gradually and continue beating until mixture holds a peak.

Green Banana Fruit Cake   Serves 12.

3 cups sifted banana
    flour°
2 cups mixed fruits
4 eggs
½ lb. butter

2 cups sugar
2 tsp. vanilla
3 tsp. baking powder
1½ cups milk

Cream butter and sugar. Add eggs and vanilla.
Blend well. Sift together flour and baking pow-
der. Add to first mixture alternately with milk.
Add fruit and mix well. Bake in moderate oven.

*Banana flour: *See* page 52.

Fancy Banana Cake   Serves 8-10.

12 ripe bananas
1 lb. flour
1 lb. sugar
3 eggs
½ lb. butter
2 tsp. vanilla

2 tsp. baking powder
1 cup honey
1 cup grapefruit juice
2 tsp. unflavoured
    gelatine
1 cup milk

Cream butter and sugar. Add eggs and blend
well. Add sifted flour and baking powder alternately with milk. Add one cup mashed banana.
Slice remaining bananas lengthwise and arrange
in greased cake tin. Mix gelatine, grapefruit
juice and honey. Boil. Pour over sliced banana.
Pour cake batter over all. Bake in oven 20 minutes at 400°F. Cool. Turn out on platter with
banana side up. Decorate with whipped cream.

Banana Tart

24 short crust pastry tart shells	3 tbs. water
	¼ cup butter
8 ripe bananas	½ cup sugar
1 tbs. lemon juice	3 tbs. rum

Peel 4 ripe bananas; slice thinly, sprinkle with lemon juice and set aside. Chop remaining bananas, place in a heavy sauce pan with 3 tablespoons water. Bring to a boil. Simmer for 10 minutes; add butter, sugar and rum. Cook slowly until thick, stirring constantly. Cool and pour into pastry shellls. Arrange sliced bananas on top. Brush with melted butter. Bake on upper shelf of oven at 375°F. for 15 minutes. Serve with cream.

Banana Caramel   Serves 8.

1 pint milk	2 tsp. vanilla
5 eggs	1 cup mashed banana
10 oz. granulated sugar	

Combine all ingredients. Pour into individual moulds which have been coated with sugar caramel. Bake in oven at 350°F. for 40 minutes. Cool. Unmould. Chill. Serve with whipped cream.

To caramelize sugar: melt slowly over low heat until sugar becomes brown in color.

42

Banana Spring   Serves 12.

3 eggs	2 tsp. baking powder
1 lb. flour	2 tsp. vanilla
1 lb. sugar	1 cup Banana Jam*
1 cup milk	1 lb. butter

Cream butter and sugar. Add eggs and vanilla. Add milk, flour and baking powder. Blend well. Bake in moderate oven. Cool. Slice in two as for layer, spread with banana jam. Decorate with whipped cream.

*Banana jam: *See* page 54.

Dressing

1 ripe banana	½ pt. whipped cream
7 strawberries or cherries	Yellow food colouring
	Lime or lemon juice

Whip cream, add lime or lemon juice and sufficient drops of coloring to make the cream a brighter color than the top of the soufflé. Spread over soufflé; garnish with banana slices and cherries.

Banana Cassata Ice Cream   Serves 12.

4 ripe bananas sliced
2 pts. vanilla ice cream
1 pt. chocolate ice
   cream

2 strips plain cake
12 small cherries
¼ cup rum

Place a layer of vanilla ice cream in the bottom of a fairly large pudding basin or an oblong pan, then a layer of cake. Pour the rum over the cake, then place another layer of vanilla ice cream on top. Arrange cherries and banana slices then top with a layer of chocolate ice cream. Freeze and turn out with chocolate layer to bottom. Slice as you would cake and serve topped with whipped cream.

Banana Coconut Delight
Serves 6.

2 ripe bananas
2 tbs. brown sugar
1 tsp. ginger
1 tsp. cinnamon
1 tbs. lime juice

1 cup grated coconut
1 pkt. lime flavoured
gelatine
1 orange

Prepare the gelatine and pour into shallow pie dish; allow to partially set. Slice bananas and arrange over gelatine, sprinkle lime juice over them. Mix together sugar, ginger and cinnamon, sprinkle over banana. Spread coconut evenly over banana. Decorate with orange segments. Refrigerate.

Honey Bananas
Serves 2-6.

Select firm ripe
bananas
Lemon juice

1 cup honey
2 tbs. water

Peel bananas, sprinkle with lemon juice. Arrange without crowding in shallow baking pan. Pour honey and water over bananas. Bake in oven at 400°F. until bananas are tender and slightly puffed, about half an hour. Baste frequently. Serve chilled or warm.

To make topping:

½ pt. whipped cream   1 doz. dates, chopped

Fold dates into whipped cream. Two or three tbs. of cognac may be added.

Banana Charlotte

Serves 8-10.

1 pkt. lemon flavored
   gelatine
20 sponge fingers or
   strips of sponge cake
7 ripe bananas
4 tbs. sugar
1 tsp. finely grated
   chocolate

1 tbs. unflavored
   nuts
½ pt. whipped cream
1 tbs. unflavored
   gelatine*
1 tbs. unflavored
1 tbs. lime juice

*Soften in a little cold water, then dissolve 1 tbs. lime juice.

Dissolve lemon-flavored gelatine in ½ pt. hot water. Add ½ cold water. Put a thin layer in bottom of mould to set. When set, cut several slices of banana and cover gelatine in mould. Pour over more gelatine, enough to cover bananas, and allow to set. Line sides of mould with sponge fingers close together. Purée remaining bananas. Add lime juice, sugar, choclate and nuts. Add whipped cream and unflavored gelatine. Mix thoroughly. Pour carefully into mould and chill for at least three hours. When ready to serve, unmould, decorate with whipped cream. Garnish with papaya or melon and banana balls, or roughly chopped gelatine.

Banana Floating Island   Serves 8.

4 egg yolks, slightly   ½ tsp. vanilla
   beaten   ½ tsp. grated lemon rind
3 tbs. sugar   1½ cups ripe banana
1½ cups milk   purée
⅛ tsp. salt

Combine egg yolks, sugar, banana and salt. Slowly stir in milk. Cook in double-boiler, stirring constantly until mixture thickens. Cool quickly. Add vanilla. Pour into dessert glasses. Chill. Make meringue and use to top mixture in glasses.

Banana Glory   Serves 6-8.

6 eggs   1 cup banana purée
1 pt. milk   1 cup grated coconut
10 oz. sugar   1 tsp. almond extract

Mix all ingredients together. Pour into mould. Place mould in a pan of water and bake for 40 minutes at 350°F. Cool and unmould. Put to chill and decorate with whipped cream.

BANANA COOKIES

Children can be delighted by banana cookie variation; and mothers know bananas provide the vitamins, minerals and the extra food energy that growing children need.

Banana-Peanut-Butter Cookies   4 dozen.

1¼ cups sifted flour
½ teaspoon baking powder
¾ teaspoon baking soda
¼ teaspoon salt
½ cup peanut butter

½ cup granulated sugar
½ cup soft shortening
½ cup brown sugar, packed
¼ cup mashed ripe banana (1 small)

Sift dry ingredients. Cream shortening, peanut butter, sugars; add banana, then flour mixture; mix well. Shape into 2″ diameter roll, and chill in refrigerator. Slice onto ungreaser cookie sheet, and bake at 375°F. for 12 minutes. Cookie batter may dropped by teaspoons on greased cookie sheet.

Banana Oatmeal Cookies   5 dozen.

¾ cup shortening
1 cup sugar
1 egg
1 cup bananas,
  mashed (3)
1 cup rolled oats
1½ cups flour

½ teaspoon soda
1 teaspoon salt
¼ teaspoon nutmeg
¾ teaspoon cinnamon
½ cup nuts, chopped,
  if desired

Cream shortening and sugar. Add egg and beat
thoroughly. Add banana, oats, nuts and blend.
Sift dry ingredients and stir into mixture. Drop
by teaspoonfuls onto greased baking sheet, 1½"
apart. Bake at 400°F. for 13-15 minutes.

BANANA PRESERVES

Crystallized Banana Peel

12 green bananas	¼ lb. granulated sugar
¾ lb. clear sugar	1 nutmeg (grated)

Peel bananas. Cut peel into strips and place in two pints of boiling water with sugar. Boil to a thick syrup. Lay out peel on a tray and sprinkle with nutmeg and sugar. Put in the sun and keep turning until all moisture is absorbed. Sprinkle with more sugar, if desired.

Banana Figs

A glass tray 2″ to 3″ deep is the best container to use. Bananas should not be dried on wood. Select firm, ripe bananas. Peel and set in rows on tray. Cover with a thin cloth and set in the sun. Turn bananas two or three times daily. Avoid breaking. Take indoors at night. Continue process for about seven days until the bananas look quite dry, brown and fully shrunken. Store in airtight containers.

Seville Orange—Banana Jelly

6 ripe seville oranges   5 ripe bananas, puréed
4 cups granulated sugar

Peel and cut oranges in quarters. Remove seeds and set them aside. Add water to cover oranges. Boil till pulpy. Strain through fine sieve. Use some of the hot liquid to soak "gum" off seeds. Strain and add to rest of liquid. Add sufficient hot water, if necessary, to yield 5 cups. Stir in sugar. Boil to syrup consistency. To each cup of hot liquid add 3 tablespoon of banana purée. Boil for 5 minutes longer. Stand glass jars in cold water; pour in hot liquid. Skim. Allow to cool.

Ginger Banana Chutney

1 lb. chopped onions   ¼ lb. crystallized ginger
6 ripe bananas put   ½ lb. raisins
    through a ricer   2 cups fruit nectar
¾ lb. chopped dates   1 tsp. salt
1½ cups vinegar   1 tsp. curry powder

To the onions, dates and bananas add vinegar and simmer 20 minutes. Add chopped ginger, salt, curry powder, raisins and nectar. Cool until thick then bottle.

51

Banana Joy   Yields 1 jar.

8 ripe bananas, puréed   3 tbs. lemon juice
1 cup granulated sugar   4 tbs. water

Mix sugar with banana purée. Stir until dissolved. Add lemon juice and water. Bring to boil, stirring frequently to prevent sticking or burning. When jelled, remove from heat and allow to stand for a few minutes. Bottle.

Banana Flour   Yields 1 lb.

20 green bananas   Juice of 3 limes

Peel and slice bananas lengthwise. Place in cold water and lime juice for 2-3 minutes. Refresh in cold water. Drain and dry. Dehydrate on tin sheet (in the sun or the oven). Grind or pound into powder. Sift. With roughage left over repeat process.

Note: The flour may be used to make puddings, porridge, dumplings, cakes.

Banana Jam

3 lbs. mashed ripe
  bananas
1½ lb. sugar

½ cup lime juice
1½ tsp. almond extract

Mix all ingredients together. Bake in hot oven for 1 hour. Allow to cool. Use as desired.

Banana and Orange Jam

6 bananas
3 oranges

1 lb. granulated sugar

Peel and slice bananas and pour strained orange juice over. Add grated rind and pulp of oranges. Add sugar. Allow to stand for 30 minutes. Bring to boil very slowly, then boil rapidly until set.

BANANA BREADS, BATTERS, SNACKS

Stay—Crisp Banana Fritters   Serves 2-4.

1 cup flour, sifted	2 teaspoons melted
2 teaspoons baking	shortening or oil
powder	2 or 3 all-yellow bananas
1¼ teaspoons salt	¼ cup flour, for coating
¼ cup sugar	Cooking oil or melted
1 egg, well beaten	fat for frying
⅓ cup milk	

For fritter batter, sift together flour, baking powder, salt and sugar. Combine egg, milk, shortening or oil. Add to dry ingredients. Mix well. Peel bananas. Cut each into 3 or 4 diagonal pieces. Roll in flour, shake off excess. Dip into batter, completely coating the banana. Fry in hot, deep fat (370°F.) 4-6 minutes, turning fritters to brown evenly. Drain. Serve hot with Passion Fruit Sauce (see page 55) and grated coconut.

Banana Pancake   Serves 6-8.

6 green bananas	1½ cups flour
3 eggs	1 tsp. nutmeg
1 onion	Salt

Peel and grate bananas. Grate onion. Mix with eggs, flour and nutmeg, adding salt to taste. Shape as for pancake and fry in hot fat until golden brown.

Passion Fruit Sauce for Fritters

½ cup sugar
1⅓ tablespoons
  cornstarch
¼ teaspoon salt
dash ground cinnamon

½ cup boiling water
2 tablespoons butter or
  margarine
⅔ cup passion fruit juice
  (or pear juice)

Mix together sugar, cornstarch, salt and cinnamon. Add water gradually. Bring to boil. Cook over medium heat until sauce is thickened, stirring constantly. Add butter or margarine and passion fruit juice. Bring to boil. Remove from heat. Serve hot. This is an excellent sauce to serve with hotcakes, baked bananas or banana shortcake.

Variation: Substitute orange and lemon juice.

Baked Green Banana Duckunoo   Serves 12.

12 green bananas
Thick milk from 1
  coconut
½ cup butter
1½ cups sugar

1 grated coconut
3 tsp. baking powder
½ cup water
1 cup mixed fruits

Peel and wash bananas in salt water to get rid of stain. Grate bananas. Add coconut milk, sugar, butter, and fruits. Mix thoroughly then add baking powder. Pour into greased cake pan and bake for 30–35 minutes. Garnish with grated coconut.

Banana Waffles

Serves 4-8.

6 ripe bananas	½ lb. sugar
3 eggs	2 tsp. baking powder
2 cups flour	Pinch of salt
½ cup milk	

Mash bananas. Add eggs and milk. Sift flour, sugar, baking powder and salt and add to mixture. Make waffles on waffle iron. Serve warm with honey or other syrup.

Banana Porridge

Serves 6.

3 green bananas
1 cup coconut cream
1 tbs. flour
½ tsp. salt
3 cups boiling water

Cinnamon
2 cups milk
1 tsp. grated nutmeg
½ tbs. vanilla
Sugar to taste

Grate bananas. Add coconut cream and beat until mixture is free from lumps. Add boiling water, salt and cinnamon. Beat again. Simmer for 20 minutes. Mix flour with about 2 tbs. water into a smooth paste. Strain. Add to mixture, stirring well. Cook for 10 minutes more. Add milk stirring until properly mixed. Remove from heat when thoroughly hot but not boiling. Add vanilla and nutmeg. Sweeten to taste. Serve garnished with thin slices of ripe banana if desired.

Banana Encante   **Serves 4.**

4 green bananas   2 tbs. coconut milk
2 tbs. margarine   2 tbs. flour
1 egg   Salt, pepper
½ tsp. baking powder

Boil green bananas. Mash while hot with margarine to moisten. Beat egg. Combine with
coconut milk, salt, baking powder, and flour.
Mix all ingredients together. Blend well. Drop
by spoonful into hot fat and fry until golden
brown. Serve with scrambled egg, or any fish
or meat dish.

Banana Hot Biscuits   **Yields 12.**

2 ripe bananas   1½ tsp. baking powder
1 tbs. lard   1½ tbs. sugar
1 cup flour   Pinch of salt

Mash bananas. Sift together flour, sugar, baking
powder and salt. Cut in lard. Make dough with
mashed bananas and flour mixture. Roll out on
floured pastry board. Cut into 2½" rounds.
Prick tops of rounds with fork and place on
greased, floured tin sheet. Bake in hot oven for
10 minutes.

Portland Muffins   Yields 12.

2¼ cups flour	1 egg beaten
3 tsp. baking powder	1 cup milk
¼ tsp. salt	4 tbs. melted butter
2 tbs. sugar	2 puréed ripe bananas

Sift flour, baking powder, salt and sugar. Mix egg, milk and melted butter. Add quickly to dry mixture and beat. Fill muffin tins with 1 tbs. batter, then 1 tbs. banana purée, then 1 tbs. batter on top. Bake for 20 to 25 minutes.

Banana Nut Bread Special

1¾ cup sifted flour	⅓ cup shortening
2¾ tsp. baking powder	⅔ cup sugar
½ tsp. salt	2 eggs
½ cup chopped nuts	1 cup ripe banana purée

Sift together flour, baking powder and salt. Add nuts. Cream shortening and sugar. Add eggs and beat well. Add flour mixture alternately with banana purée, blending thoroughly after each addition. Pour into 9″ loaf pan. Bake in oven at 350°F. for one hour. Let bread cool in pan before turning out.

Banana Bread

This is a specialty banana-flavored quick bread with moist, cakelike texture. Serve plain or toasted for breakfast, luncheon, or dinner.

1¾ cups flour, sifted
2¾ teaspoons baking powder (double action)
½ teaspoon salt

⅓ cup shortening
⅔ cup sugar
2 eggs
3 or 4 ripe bananas

Sift together flour, baking powder and salt. Beat shortening in mixer bowl until creamy. Add sugar and eggs. Continue beating at medium speed 1 minute (or 150 strokes by handbeater). Peel bananas. Add to egg mixture. Mix until blended. Add flour mixture, beating at low speed for 30 seconds, or only until blended. *Do not overbeat.*

Scrape bowl and beater once or twice. Turn into greased loaf pan and bake in a moderate oven (350°F.) about 1 hour and 10 minutes or until bread is done.

Variations: To egg mixture add either: 1 cup coarsely chopped nuts; 1 cup seedless raisins, or 1 cup finely chopped dates.

BANANA BEVERAGES

Banana Daiquiri   Serves 6.

2 ripe bananas   6 oz. sugar
4 oz. lime juice   8 oz. rum

Place ingredients in blender with cracked ice and blend well. Garnish as desired.

Banana-Orange Fruit Shake   Serves 2.

1 ripe banana   ½ cup orange juice
1 cup ginger ale

Purée banana. Add orange juice. Shake until smooth and creamy. Mix in ginger ale. Chill well or serve over cracked ice.

Banana Wine

1 lb. dates   6 ripe bananas in their
½ lb. rice   skins
5 qts. water   2 ozs. liquid tea
                              4 lbs. sugar

Cut bananas crosswise in the skin. Put dates, rice and bananas in water to simmer for 15 minutes. Add the tea and boil for 5 minutes. Strain. Add sugar and stir till dissolved. Place in an earthenware jar and cover. Let it ripen for about 30 days and then bottle. Pour off into new bottles as sediment settles and keep doing this until the wine is clear.

Banana Milk Shake
Serves 3.

2 - 3 ripe bananas
1 pt. milk
½ tsp. vanilla

¼ teaspoon bitters
Sugar to taste
Food coloring, if desired

Purée bananas. Add sugar, milk, salt, vanilla and bitters. Blend well. Serve over cracked ice.

Banana Delight
Serves 6.

1 ripe banana
16 oz. can mango
   (or pear) nectar

1 jigger rum
1 lime

Pureé all bananas but one. Add nectar and rum to pureé. Mix well. Dice remaining banana; add to mixture. Serve over cruched ice. Garnish with lime slices.

Frappé De Strength
Serves 4.

4 ripe bananas
½ pt. milk
½ tin sweetened
   condensed milk

2 tbs. sugar
½ tsp. vanilla
Salt
Nutmeg

Mash bananas. Add the milk and rub mixture through strainer. Add salt, nutmeg. Add vanilla, condensed milk and sugar. Blend well with crushed ice. Serve in old fashioned glasses with straw.

Banana Nectar
Serves 3.

6 ripe bananas
Juice of 3 large limes
Sugar to taste

Peel bananas, rub through sieve or blend in food blender. Add sugar and lime juice. Blend again. Blend with cracked ice before serving.

West Indies Banana Drink   Serves 12.

6 ripe bananas	¾ lb. sugar
1 qt. milk	1 tsp. vanilla
1 can sweetened con-	½ tsp. nutmeg
densed milk	6 tbs. sherry
1 can evaporated milk	Dash of cinnamon

Mash bananas well; add sugar and nutmeg. Beat well. Add evaporated and condensed milk. Beat again. Add the milk, vanilla, sherry and cinnamon. Strain through a fine sieve. Serve cold.

Mococo Banana Punch   Serves 12.

6 ripe bananas	3 eggs
1 pt. milk	1 tsp. nutmeg
1 can condensed milk	2 - 3 oz. brandy
1 tsp. vanilla	

Purée bananas. Beat eggs and combine with purée. Add the milk, condensed milk, vanilla, nutmeg and brandy. Place all ingredients in blender over cracked ice. Blend well.

Banana Special   Serves 1.

¼ of a ripe banana	3 oz. liquid sugar
1 oz. lime juice	Soda water

Purée banana. Add lime juice and sugar. Blend well with crushed ice. Pour into 10 oz. glass, fill with soda water.

www.ingramcontent.com/pod-product-compliance
Lightning Source LLC
Chambersburg PA
CBHW010859090426
42738CB00018B/3448